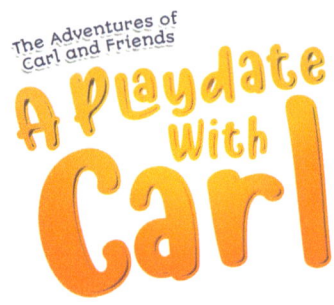

Published by Tamekia Parence
Atlanta, GA

Library of Congress Control Number: 2021907991

Copyright © 2021 by Tamekia Parence

All Rights Reserved. No part of this publication may be reproduced or transmitted in any form or by any means, electronic or mechanical, including photocopying and recording, or by any information storage or retrieval system without written permission from the copyright owner.
Printed in the United States of America
ISBN-13: 978-1-7366965-2-1

Editing, Illustrations, Book Cover Design, Layout, & Formatting by DG Self-Publishing
www.dgselfpublishing.com

APlayDateWithCarl.com
: aplaydatewithcarl

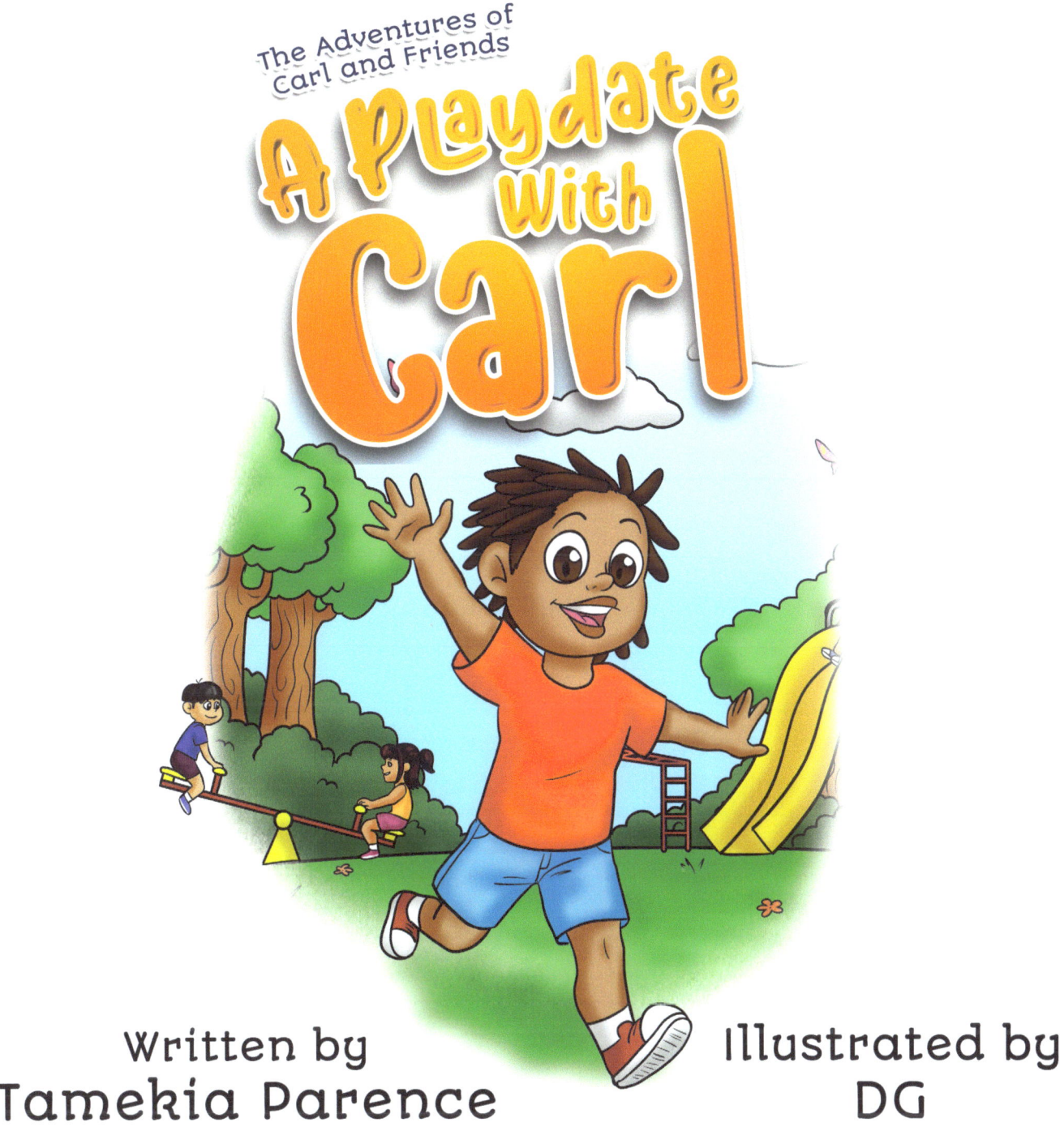

Dedication

This book is dedicated to my son, Carl Mumford III. May you always shine light, spread love, and be the best person you can be.

Love,

Mommy

"Mommy, will you come play with me?" asked Carl.
"Sure, baby. What do you want to play?" Mommy replied.
"Let's play cowboys and cowgirls. I'll be Woody, and you can be Jessie."
"Ok."

"Mommy, look!" said Carl. "There's a big truck outside." "I see. Looks like we have new neighbors moving in. We will go over and welcome them once they are all settled in," said Mommy.

The next morning after breakfast, Carl couldn't wait to go meet the new neighbors.

"Mommy, Mommy, can we go see the neighbors now?" he asked.

"Sure, baby. Let's finish cleaning up from breakfast, and we will go over there this afternoon," Mommy promised.

Later that day, Carl and his mommy went across the street to the new neighbors' house.

"Hello, my name is Tamekia, and this is my son Carl," said Mommy. "We wanted to welcome you and your family to the neighborhood. We live right across the street."

"Oh, thank you!" said the woman who answered the door.

"I'm Monica, and this is my son Trevor. My daughter Jasmine is unpacking upstairs. We just moved here from Tennessee."

"Would you like to come play with me?" Carl asked Trevor. Trevor turned to his mother. "Mom, can I?"

"Sure, if it's ok with you, Tamekia?"

"Sure!" said Carl's mommy. "Come on, boys. Let's go back across the street so Ms. Monica can finish unpacking. I'll bring him back before dark."

"Ok, sounds good. Have fun, boys!" Trevor's mom said with a smile.

Carl and Trevor had fun playing all afternoon. They played with trucks, played hide-and-seek, and ran around all day. Then it came time for Trevor to go back home.

Carl walked Trevor to his house. When they reached Trevor's front door,

Carl said, "See you later, Trevor. Have a good night."

Trevor said, "Ok, bye."

The next day, Trevor came over to see if Carl would like to play with him.

But when Carl came to the door, he was in a wheelchair, and his leg was wrapped up.

Trevor said, "Oh no! What happened? You can't play with me like that!"

Carl said, "Yes, I can!"

Carl's mom appeared behind him. She explained to Trevor and Ms. Monica that Carl has a condition called osteogenesis imperfecta (OI), also known as brittle bone disease.

"With this condition, Carl's bones can break very easily, like if you were to break a small, thin stick," Carl's mom said.

"Last night, Carl hurt his leg getting ready for bed. He fractured his femur and must wear a splint and use his wheelchair until his leg heals."

Carl said, "We can still play together, Trevor. We can play catch, blow bubbles, play hide-and-seek—we can play everything we did yesterday. Even though I have to use my wheelchair, we can still have fun just like we did before."

Trevor said, "Oh, really? . . . Ok!"
"Yeah, and look how cool my chair is with my light-up wheels!" said Carl as he wheeled around in circles to show them off. Trevor said, "Wow! That's cool!"